First Edition

www.ahavapress.com

Photograph of Nikki and her piglets used by permission
From Farm Sanctuary, Watkins Glen, NY.

ISBN 978-0-615-46576-0

Lucky Pigs ©Susan Rooker 2011

Lucky Pigs

For Ben & Max…and Nikki

Nikki knew what was about to happen.

By the shimmering dots of light poking

through the darkening sky and by the animals returning

from their day in the pasture, she could predict it.

"Mama, tell us the story," cried Freston, snuggling next to Nikki for warmth.

"Oh my, Sweetie. You've heard it so many times," Nikki replied, smiling as pigs often do.

This was exactly what she had expected.

"But we like it! We like it!" clamored the
other piglets, Portia, Ellen, Chuck, and Rory.

"All right, all right.

Then it's right to bed.

OK," Nikki began. " Long ago, in a horrible place far, far
away, I lived – if you can call it that.
My life was miserable…"

"You slept on a hard cold floor!" Ellen interrupted.

"Yes, and..."

"...and your trotters hurt," Chuck added.

"You never saw the sun and the food was terrible."

"It gave you tummy aches."

"That's right, and..."

"And you were about to have babies."

"And that place was smelly and noisy."

"Yes, and I…"

"You were going to have us!" They giggled.

"That's right. And I…"

"You shouted, 'Please give me something soft to lie on!' "
Ellen continued, "and you yelled 'Please give me
more room!' " Rory cried, "but no one heard you."

"Yes. But then…"

"But then it started to rain?"

"That's right.

It started to rain."

"It rained...

and rained...

and rained.

It rained so much that

brooks swelled to rivers.

Rivers ran over their banks.

Flat farmlands turned into

muddy lakes.

Then I"…

"Oh-oh-oh!" said Freston excitedly. "suddenly the metal doors of your crate and the huge doors of the factory swung open!"
"You were free!

Free!

Free!

FR---EEEEE!"
Ellen sang.

Rory continued, "You swam in that thick mucky mud. You searched for a safe spot to stay.

Your back ached. Your trotters split.

Then you found a high
mound of dry ground!"

"You had your babies!"

"'Your babies were us!"
declared the piglets.

"But what happened then, Mama?"
asked Rory.

"Yeah, Mama. What happened next?"

"Well, next...

we waited and waited, and..."
"And you thought, 'Oh no. Now what will I do to keep my new babies warm and fed?' " Freston said quietly.

"And you didn't know it *but…*" whispered Rory.

"...there was a group of people looking for pigs like you who'd escaped that crowded smelly place."

"Yes," Nikki nodded. "I heard them talking."

Portia said, "You heard them say,

'Hey, look over there!

Five babies… and there's the mother!' "

"The rescuers worked together," added Nikki, "leading us to a truck and out of the squishy squashy mud."

"And what did *we* do, Mama?
What did *we* do then?" whispered Ellen.
"Do?" asked Nikki.
"Well, you followed me and asked…"

"I asked, 'Where are we going, Mama?' "
Chuck grinned, knowing the story well,
"And you said, 'Good question!
I don't know.' "

…"But I've got a good feeling! So
let's go! " shouted the other piglets.

"And did we go, Mama?
Did we? Did we go?"

"We sure did," Nikki said. " We climbed into the back of a truck and cuddled in the dry straw. The road was bumpy and the trip was long. Finally, the truck stopped.

The doors opened wide to let us out.

One by one, as slowly as can be,

we stepped out of that truck.

And what did we see?"

"A farm! A real farm!
with grass so green,
tall trees and red barns,
with turkeys and ducks,
and soft chicks who cluck,
cows who mmmooooo
And yes! Yes!
Pigs who oink too!"

"And we cried, 'Hooray!' "

"And Mama, you yelled, 'Yippee!

We're home! Come on out!

It's safe!' "

"We loved the big sky above and
sweet smells around.

You knew, at last, a home we'd found."

"We love that story.
You are a great storyteller, Mama!"

At last, the five tired piglets
cuddled in close to
Nikki and slowly, slowly
drifted
        off
            to
                sleep.

Nikki smiled, as pigs often do.

You see, the story she told was true.

Her piglets, she guessed, did not think the same.

Perhaps they thought it was just a game.

Nikki did not care nor mind.

because her troubles were far behind.

Their lives would be happy and carefree

lived out long in this farm sanctuary.

Photo courtesy of Farm Sanctuary

About Nikki
Nikki *is a real pig*. She and her five piglets were rescued from a dry patch of land during the floods that ravaged Iowa farmlands during Summer 2008.

"Lucky Pigs" captures the events as reported by rescuers on site. Nikki, Freston, Rory, Ellen, Portia, and Chuck live happily and free at Farm Sanctuary, Watkins Glen, New York.

For more information about Farm Sanctuary www.farmsactuary.org.

www.ingramcontent.com/pod-product-compliance
Lightning Source LLC
Chambersburg PA
CBHW042151290326

41934CB00002BA/59

* 9 7 8 0 6 1 5 4 6 5 7 6 0 *